The Little
Book of
Zen

To my family:
Angus, Marléne and Lettie.

The Little Book of Zen

Émile Marini

Contents

Introduction: Why Zen?

Before you read another word, ask yourself this: what did you hope to find in this book?

What did you hope to find in *The Little Book of Zen*? What drew you to this little paperback? What made you open it? What did you hope might be here?

These questions aren't idle: they matter. They matter for two reasons:

1 They matter because the journey that brought you here is as important as where you're going, and

2 Because the word 'Zen' has been used to mean so many things over the last thousand years that it's worth making sure – right now, before we get into anything – that we're on the same page.

Plus, Zen is *all* questions.

To live a Zen life is a constant search for the truth; any search for the truth must, by *its* nature, involve questioning even those things of which we were most certain.

What Is Zen?

The most simple (and common) way to define Zen is as *a branch of Buddhism that focuses mostly on enlightenment, particularly achieving enlightenment through meditation and intuition.* While this may seem simple enough, there's actually lots to unpack: what do you know about Buddhism? What actually is 'enlightenment'? How do you 'meditate' in a way that's meaningful, and how can we learn to grapple with our own 'intuition' in a way that's clear and useful to us?

We'll get to each of these questions in due course, but first we need to acknowledge that this definition of Zen is, well, *sometimes wrong.* It's not always wrong. It's not even mostly wrong. But Zen means many different things to many different people, and essentially always has. Zen has many different schools, and many different approaches, and this book – all books – must always be a compromise.

The cultural appropriation (and reimagining) of the concept of Zen is almost as old as Zen itself: it came first from the Sanskrit *dhyana* (see page 37), shaded through the Chan School of Buddhism in China, was popularized in Korea 13 centuries ago and, at last, was filtered through Western psychoanalysis, spiritualism and inescapable capitalism. There is much talk, in discussion of Zen, about 'authenticity', and if this appeals to you, this is not the Zen book for you. In fact, if 'authenticity' matters to you, there is no Zen book for you. Zen, in its purest form, is supposed to be between student and teacher alone; between two people, one a master and one a novice. The idea, to a strict Zen Buddhist, of a book being a substitute for real communion is laughable. And yet, here we are.

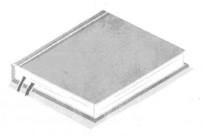

About This Book

This is not a guide to Buddhism, that ancient and complex religion, but it does use many of the ideas of Buddhism – and throughout the book (on pages 34, 50, 68 and 82), you'll find short sections explaining the key pillars of Buddhism. This is because to approach Zen without Buddhism would be to strip it of context, meaning and power.

It is also not a guide, strictly speaking, to Zen itself. It is a guide to using the tools and principles of Zen to make our lives better, simpler, easier. It is a guide to allowing the benefits of Zen into our daily lives in such a way as is practical for us in the here and now; to not allowing a quest for perfection to override a daily effort for things to be just a little better.

Let Me Tell You a Story

This book is full of stories – sometimes called 'koans'– told from master to student and repeated for many centuries. From each story we can learn something, and often something new each time; sometimes it takes years, decades to understand what a story means. Koans are something to meditate on, something to think about. Sometimes they are funny. Sometimes they are bizarre or grotesque. Sometimes they are unsettling. Sometimes they seem to make no sense at all. All have meaning, somewhere. All have something in them to unpack.

The story on the following pages is not a koan, but without this story there are no koans; no Zen at all. This is the story of the Buddha, and how the Buddha came to be.

There was once, a long time ago, a prince. He was deeply beloved, this prince, and above all he was loved by his father.

His father was a powerful king, and wanted his son to know nothing of unhappiness. The king gave his son everything he could want, and he kept from his son anything that could harm him. The king loved his son, and so, too, he kept from him anything that might take the boy away from the gilded gates of the castle. He kept from him anything that might take the boy away from the path the king wanted him to follow, and anything that might bring him sorrow. Even the sick and the old were sent away that the prince should not learn of their existence, and so grieve.

Everything in the palace was young and whole and beautiful, and the prince had everything. And he should have been happy, and perhaps he was, for a time. But people are not made to live behind gates, even gilded ones, and so one night – following some unnamed impulse, maybe – the prince went out into the world, and there the prince saw, for the first time – people.

He saw four people, on four nights, and one of the people was dead. That was the third thing he saw: a dead man, and he had not even known of the existence of death before that. The first night he saw an old man, twisted and broken by time, and he had not even known of age, he had not known of sickness; and on the second night he saw a sick man. Imagine. He asked his servant to tell him, please, what had happened to these people.

And the servant told him: this happens to all men. This suffering is the fate of all men.

And the prince saw that it was true.

On the fourth night he saw a hermit, who had given up all his life to find the cause of these sufferings; and on the fourth night the prince went out of the gilded gates, to follow the hermit, and he did not return. He went to live among the people, and of the people, and to try to find a cure for the sickness and the suffering and the age and the death.

Or, at least, to find a reason for it.

This Is Your Zen

The story on the previous pages is, more or less, the story of the Buddha: it is, more or less, the origin story of Buddhism, and although this is not a book about Buddhism *qua* Buddhism, it *is* a book about people. The Buddha did not begin his story in the world, but he went into the world;

the Buddha's life was not one of retreat into an ivory tower, but of a decision to go into the world among the people, among the suffering, among the real things of life. The story of the Buddha is not separate from the world, from the way we live, but of it. It is for that reason that we not only *can* but *must* bring the tools and techniques of Zen into our own ordinary, messy human lives.

To think and write about Zen in such a way as to make it accessible and indeed helpful to our ordinary lives, we must rid ourselves of the impossible idea of perfection. We must rid ourselves of the idea that there is one true way of practising Zen – the way of the shaved head and orange robe – and instead embrace Zen as a lens through which to view our whole lives, to make the ordinary extraordinary: a lens through which we can see, to quote William Blake, 'a World in a Grain of Sand/And a Heaven in a Wild Flower'. Zen is about, maybe, seeing clearly: we see first ourselves, and then our world, and then our place within it.

'All beings by nature are Buddha/as ice by nature is water,'
wrote the great Zen philosopher Hakuin Ekaku in the 18th
century. This belongs to us: to all of us, and so the spirit of
Zen can be as much here in this little book – in the
bookstore or at home on your sofa or on the bus – as
anywhere. This is your book, your life, your Zen. This is for
you who thought, maybe, that you would never achieve Zen
in a more conventional sense. This is for you who picked up
this book, and hoped for something more. This is for you
who hoped.

1

The Overflowing Teacup

and the Beginner's Mind

Once there was a rich man who had everything he could possibly need. There was nothing he could not buy, and he was used to getting everything he wanted, and everything his own way.

One day he heard of a great Zen master, and went to him. 'Open my mind to enlightenment,' he told the Zen master. 'Teach me.' He was, remember, used to getting everything he wanted. He was used to getting things his own way.

The master smiled, told the man to sit down and called for tea. When the tea was served, the master set a cup before the rich man and began to pour. The master kept pouring. He kept pouring, and the tea came up to the rim of the cup and over the rim. 'You're spilling it,' said the rich man, but the master kept pouring, and the tea came onto the table. 'What are you doing?' said the rich man, but the master kept pouring and the tea flooded the table. 'The cup is full!' cried the rich man. 'Stop! Stop pouring!' But the master did not stop, and the tea spilled onto the expensive robes of the

rich man. 'Can't you see the cup is full?' cried the
rich man. 'What are you doing?'

'You are the cup,' said the master, still smiling.
'You are the cup, so full that nothing more can be
added. Come back to me with an empty mind,
and I can teach you.'

A Full Teacup

When we come to begin any form of study, we come with our prejudices and our preconceptions. We come with an idea of what we might be about to learn, and where that learning journey might take us. I'd bet that right now, you have a few ideas about what Buddhism is, what Zen is and how they can help you – as discussed in the Introduction to this book. After all, wherever we go, we bring everything we are, and everything we have accumulated over the years, with us; we are an amalgam of every idea we've picked up and absorbed throughout our lives.

'*Cogito, ergo sum,*' wrote the philosopher René Descartes: *I think, therefore I am.* He meant that in order for a thought to exist, there has to be someone to think it; the idea of the thought proves the existence of the thinker. But we can also take this to mean that we are intrinsically linked with our thoughts. Our thoughts make us who we are, and make up our sense

of how we live. Some of these thoughts are sensible and based in reality; some of them are speculations, or based on false premises. Some of them are feelings. Some of them are assumptions. Some of them start from ideas that aren't necessarily helpful. We are a million things, made of contradictions, desires, sufferings and dreams – and we are, in short, starting with a pretty full teacup.

Let me be clear: this isn't an accusation, or an attack. A full teacup is the human condition. A full teacup is everyone's starting point (not just a rich man in a Zen koan), and this is not necessarily a bad thing. It's not a bad thing provided we don't mind doing the work to empty the teacup – to empty our minds – and, in fact, that's exactly what this book is for. We empty the teacup so that we can see what the teacup really is: who we really are.

Because we are, according to Zen tradition, already enlightened. We are already enough; we already know the answers. We aren't trying to find something external, but something internal: some truth simultaneously fundamental to ourselves and common to all. The great American master

Charlotte Joko Beck once described Zen as the process of 'becoming acquainted with ourselves'. Every other benefit that comes with this practice is perhaps ultimately a by-product of this extreme self-knowledge. To know yourself is to know the context in which you exist; to know the context in which you exist is to know the world; to know the world as it really is is to be kinder, more thoughtful and more aware. Who knows? It may even make you happier.

Take a Moment to Notice

So where to begin? We begin by *acknowledging*
our preconceptions; we begin by acknowledging
ourselves where we are, by meeting ourselves at our
current state.

Take a moment, now, to notice where you are,
emotionally and physically; notice any worries, or
any stresses. You might want to write these down.
Notice how you feel about this book, and this exercise;
notice if anything has spoken to you so far, and notice
(it's fine!) if it hasn't. Notice yourself – even if, right
now, all you can be sure of is where you are. Where are
you, right now? How are you sitting? How are you
standing? Are you in any pain or discomfort? Are you
slouching or holding yourself up straight? How are
your core muscles and your spine? How do you *feel*?

Don't try to change things, unless you want to;
don't feel you have to be different.

The Beginner's Mind

We can't try to be what we are not, and we can't try to get somewhere without knowing where we begin. In the following chapters, and in time, we'll delve into practical methods of meditation, communion and connection; we'll speak of the Buddha, his teachings and the Three Jewels (or Three Treasures) of Zen Buddhism. We'll talk about our influences and our actions; about the Noble Eightfold Path and the Three Pure Precepts. We'll learn about how to incorporate the attitudes and directions of Zen into our ordinary lives, a little at a time, and whether a regular life in an increasingly capitalist and corporate society can, in fact, ever be Zen. (We will also talk about whether this kind of puritan attitude is remotely helpful; and, indeed, if this ascetic strictness does more harm than good.)

And perhaps some of these ideas are already familiar to you. Perhaps you already know something of these things, and yet in order to come through this little book – and any kind of Zen study – we must come with what's known as the Beginner's Mind, or *shoshin*. We must come humble, with an empty teacup, ready to receive anything as if for the first time. We must come ready to receive whatever life gives us; ready and receptive to understand the lessons that life is teaching us. You see, we must come to Zen with *shoshin* in order that we may come to everything else in our life with *shoshin*.

This sounds like another koan in and of itself – but the truth is that this is the way that Zen is not merely a part of, but a whole approach to, life. Zen is not something we can pick up and put down; it is a state of mind by which we approach all our own decisions, our own actions, our own relationships and our own feelings. Zen is life; and life, done right, is Zen.

We'll end this chapter with a quick exercise, drawn from mindfulness therapies. It might seem a little strange, but go with it: I promise you it's leading up to something.

This exercise is inspired, too, by the work of British food writer Bee Wilson. Wilson works extensively with an organization called Taste Education, who believe that obesity can be tackled by teaching children to eat mindfully and carefully: they routinely take fruits and vegetables into schools, and ask children to play with them, taste them, touch them, feel them, observe them, describe them. They believe that it is vital to the human experience to eat with attention: to bring, in a sense, the Beginner's Mind to this also.

The Raisin Exercise

You'll need, for this exercise, a few raisins. Raisins, like the dried-fruit, packed-lunch snack kind of raisins. Ordinary raisins.

(Raisins are great because there's a lot to *notice* about them, and they have the benefit of feeling already familiar to most of us. If you can't get raisins, feel free to use any other food. Try dates, dried apricots or walnuts as alternatives. And, as we progress through this book, we'll come back to the skills we're first attempting here with everything we eat. We're learning attention exercises here that, in time, we'll bring to every element of our lives.)

Hold the raisins in your hand.

Now imagine – really, as hard as you can – that you have *never seen a raisin before*. You have never heard of this food. You have never come across anything like this. You have never seen a raisin before. This? You have no idea what this is. You have no idea what's in your hand.

One at a time, I want you to bring each of your senses to bear on the raisins: look, touch, sound, smell, taste.

What does it look like? What does its skin look like? How big is it? How does it feel in your hand? Does it have a smell? What does it taste like? What does it feel like in your mouth? What is the texture, and is it different when you touch it and when you taste it?

Eat the raisin mindfully, slowly, with concentration. Jot down a few notes, perhaps. Really focus your mind on this raisin, as if you're preparing a report for someone else who has also never eaten a raisin.

Take your time. Eat another raisin with the same degree of conscious attention. Don't let your mind wander off topic: tell me about the raisin. Write your notes about the raisin. Keep your mind on the raisin. Imagine you're a scientist, exploring the possibilities inherent in the raisin.

Maybe this exercise, especially the imaginative parts, seemed very silly to you. If so, I'm sorry — perhaps it is — but I want you to try it anyway. You don't have to tell anyone, and I won't if you don't.

You see, this kind of play, and possibility for play, is inherent to a Zen way of looking at life. Sometimes looking at the world through a playful lens gives us a whole new way of understanding that which seemed mundane or routine before — and that is right at the heart of Zen.

What we're doing with this exercise is learning to focus our attention rigorously on a single thing — and we're doing this for two reasons.

First, as practice: we want to be able to train our minds not to wander. We want to be able to direct our attention fully to a single thing, and a single purpose, as and when we see fit. We want to be able to be the master of our own minds, rather than being dragged hither and thither by the whims of our imaginative and distracted inner monologues.

But second, did you notice that while you were concentrating on the raisin – if you did it right – there was no space left in your mind at that moment for conscious worry about anything else? Think about those worries and stresses we acknowledged a little earlier in this chapter. Did you think of them while you were contemplating the raisin? Or did it buy you just a little moment of peace? This is the point of meditation – not to give you space to obsess over your worries, but to give you space from them – and it's meditation to which we'll turn in the next chapter.

The Eightfold Path

These are the eight steps at the heart of Buddhism,
the eight central tenets by which Buddhists live.
By holding to these principles we can be freed,
so Buddhists believe, from the ancient and eternal
cycle of suffering.

The cycle is called *samsara*, and it means repetition.
It means doing the same things again. It means
'wandering', as in wandering through a desert,
as in wandering without direction. It means
aimlessness: a life without purpose, an existence
without beginning or end, a world without
meaning. By these eight steps we can be freed.
By these steps we can find, at last, peace: nirvana.

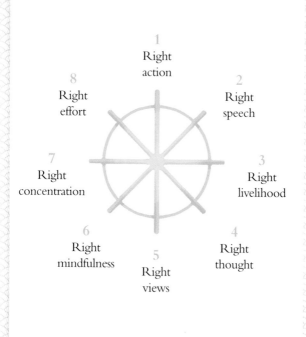

1
Right
action

2
Right
speech

8
Right
effort

3
Right
livelihood

7
Right
concentration

4
Right
thought

6
Right
mindfulness

5
Right
views

2

A Practical Guide to Meditation

If our minds were simple enough to understand, they say, we would be too simple to understand them: a paradox worthy of being a Zen koan in and of itself. We solve this riddle – as we solve all Zen riddles – through meditation.

You almost certainly have some preconceived ideas about meditation: your teacup is probably spilling over as we speak. For a start, I suspect you think it's very difficult – or very boring. In fact, true meditation is neither. True meditation is a process, not a perfected act – and it's one you can start right now, exactly where you are. It is simply the act of training your attention to go where you want it to go, of focusing the mind as it should best be focused and of achieving some kind of mental clarity.

'Meditation' is the best English translation for two Sanskrit words and concepts: *bhavana* and *dhyana*.

Dhyana is 'the training of the mind', and is one of the oldest concepts of Buddhism. It comes from the ancient Indo-European word for contemplation – and it's actually the root for the Japanese word Zen itself.

Bhavana means 'development', and it comes from the Sanskrit for 'becoming'. It's often said to be related to the word for 'cultivation', like a farmer might cultivate a field – and as Harvard scholar Glenn Wallis has noted, it's a very ordinary word. It's a word that belongs to the people: it's a word that suggests planting seeds and digging rows and doing your best with what you have. It's a word that implies work and care and diligence.

There are many things to say about meditation – and much that's been said over the centuries – but this chapter, before we delve any further into the tenets of Buddhism or the theories of Zen, is simply a practical guide.

By finding a sense of physical calm and stillness, we create the environment for mental calm and stillness. Having an awareness of the physical body allows us to create an awareness of our mental state: by seeing and understanding our place in the world, we understand much better how we might go about fitting in to it, rather than struggling in vain to fit the world around us. We can change nothing but ourselves; and without an understanding of ourselves, therefore, can change nothing.

To study the way
is to study the self.

To study the self
is to forget the self.

– Zen master
Eihei Dōgen

How to Sit to Meditate

The famous *Yoga Sutras* – written by the sage Patanjali
at least 1,500 years ago – have a complex relationship to
Buddhism and Zen well beyond the scope of this book.
While worth exploring in more detail for the more
advanced Zen scholar, there's only one phrase we need
to note here: sutra 2.46, *sthira sukham asanam*. This sutra is
usually translated as something like 'seated position should
be steady and comfortable', and we're going to unpack these
three words now to give us some ancient tips on how, simply,
to sit – and how to sit to meditate. You see, 'meditation' can
also be translated as the simple word *zazen*. This Japanese
word means seated meditation, and most Zen meditation
(the clue is in the name) is zazen.

Zazen is at the heart of becoming Zen, or living Zen: the
sitting, and the stillness, that act as both practice and reward,
both journey and destination. As the Buddha sat, so we can
sit. (Or, for the sake of clarity, whatever posture is possible
for your body.)

Asanam

Asanam is fairly simple: like *zazen*, it means seat, and sitting.
We tend to sit cross-legged when we meditate. We do this
because it's the most stable posture, whether it is cross-legged
in the lotus position, or simply 'criss-cross applesauce'
(known in this context as 'Burmese style'). The lotus
position, familiar (as much of this will be) to yoga devotees,
can be a little tricky to master – but, once mastered, provides
a stable, comfortable way to sit for long periods of time. It's
important to note that the lotus position is very much not
suitable for everybody – and how the position looks is much
less important than how it *feels*. (Feel free to use a cushion or
a folded blanket here to stabilize your position.)

Have your eyes open, and your gaze soft; turn your palms
out to the universe, to show, even just to yourself, that you're
ready to receive what it wants to bring you. Know where
your hands are; feel where you are against the floor, or
wherever you've chosen to rest for this time.

Sthira

Sthira means steadiness; it means commitment, it means consistency. It means showing up. It means being able to stay as we are for a long time: finding a way of being that allows us to sit, as we did with the Raisin Exercise on page 30, with ourselves; and to fully concentrate on both the self and the lack of self. (We're going to explore this duality further in Chapter 3 – don't worry if it seems a bit mad so far!) What it means practically is that we shouldn't sit somewhere where we're going to be interrupted; it means don't try to choose, for example, a complex posture that we can't hold, or force ourselves into a lotus position we aren't comfortable maintaining.

Sukham

Sukham is translated as 'a space of ease': a place of comfort,
a sense of freedom even when we're going nowhere. Think
of those two words as you settle into your seat. Space, ease:
these are words that give grace to our cross-legged position.
You might associate sitting cross-legged with childhood, and
while we absolutely want to bring that sense of playful
experimentation – of doing what feels good; of finding a
way to exist in our bodies that feels good as children do
instinctively – we also need to understand the great and
lasting dignity of sitting *zazen*. When we sit in this way,
we sit in a long tradition of people attempting to find
clarity the whole world over, for thousands of years, in many
different traditions. We form part of a vast chain of human

connection, all striving for something more than themselves. Or the same as themselves. (We'll look at this in the next chapter. Again, don't worry!)

Sukham can also mean, according to some experts, 'towards the sky', and it's the way these two words intertwine that gives a whole new meaning to the phrase. Yogi Rima Rabbath has written extensively on what it means to be both solid and spacious, both consistently grounded and also reaching for the sky. She compares it, in fact, to the moment before a bird takes flight: poised and ready. In this way, we are ready, when we sit *zazen*. We are ready for the universe, and the universe is ready to accept us.

We're going to move now to an exercise that will be familiar to those who practise yoga: a simple breath attention exercise.

Breath Attention

Sit comfortably, as on page 42, and bring your shoulders back. Try to make your shoulderblades kiss a little in the middle and engage your core muscles (pretend you want your belly button to meet your spine). This is just good posture – nothing fancy!

Be, in this position, as still as you can.

Breathe normally.

Observe your breath – without judgement. Don't try to change it or modulate it. You're fine as you are. We have to meet ourselves where we are to see ourselves clearly. All we're doing here is observing our natural state. This is about noticing your normal: about being mindful of every breath we put into the world.

Ask yourself:

- How does the breath feel in my mouth and my nose? How about in my chest?

- How does the breath feel in my lungs? Is it reaching every part of my lungs, or just the top?

- How does the breath feel in my throat? Is it cold or hot? Does it hurt at all?

- How does my body feel when I breathe in? How does my body feel when I breathe out?

Let the mind follow the breath; and let our attention follow the breath. The breath is the spirit, and the breath is life. The Zen teacher Dainin Katagiri, in his book *Returning to Silence*, says that human life is like a ball, and the breath is the still centre of the ball. Find your still centre. Find your heart.

We notice the breath because it provides an easy rhythm for us to follow; an easy route into the self in a world where the self is often overridden by louder voices. You see how even in the exercise on the previous page, we can use the breath as a vehicle to notice the body; to draw our attention to our lungs, our throat, our nose and mouth. To observe the self, remember, is to observe the universe. Within us we contain whole worlds, and the whole miracle of creation —whatever you believe – exists within us. Follow the breath; follow the self; see the self in the context of a wild and swirling universe where so much is possible.

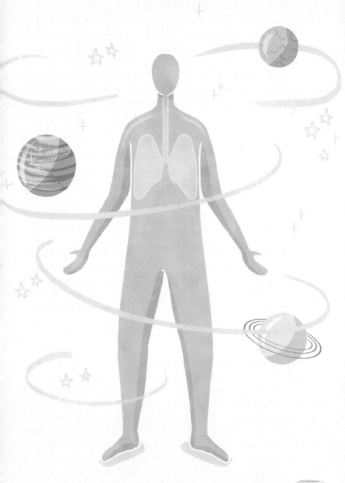

The Three Jewels

The Three Jewels, sometimes called the Three
Treasures, are the three most sacred things in
Buddhism: the three things in which you can take
solace and find peace. They are the three pillars, if
you like, on which you can lean and to which you
can return. In Zen we come back to these three
things as somewhere to 'find refuge'. Beneath are
written three ways of expressing these Three
Jewels: in the Pali language and the Theravada
Buddhist tradition, to start, and then (in a little
more detail) the Mahayana Buddhist tradition.

Buddham saranam gacchāmi.

I go for refuge in the Buddha.

*I take refuge in the Buddha, wishing for all
sentient beings to understand the great Way
profoundly and make the greatest resolve.*

Dhammam saranam gacchãmi.

I go for refuge in the Dharma.

*I take refuge in the Dharma [the lessons
and teachings of Zen] wishing for all sentient
beings to delve deeply into the Sutra Pitaka
[texts of the Buddhist canon], causing their
wisdom to be as broad as the sea.*

Sangham saranam gacchãmi.

I go for refuge in the Sangha.

*I take refuge in the Sangha [the community
around me], wishing for all sentient beings to
lead the congregation in harmony, entirely
without obstruction.*

3

The Moon in Water

and Understanding
What We Can't
Understand

Part of the problem with beginning to study Zen, particularly in a Western context, is that it is *in essence* both very simple and immensely complex. Zen is a search for the truth of all nature; of all desire, of all suffering, of all humanity and even all existence. In the West, we are pretty used to having a good idea of what we're going after before we go about getting it – and Zen simply doesn't work like that. Usually when we start to learn something, we have a rough idea of what we might know by the end – and what we might know at the end of a lifetime of Zen is unteachable by anything but experience. Zen is a way of life; a series of small revelations, one after the other, about what it is to exist in the world as the world exists.

'Not knowing' is sometimes said, in Zen, to be the truest relationship anyone can have with anything; and it's also said to be the closest, most intimate relationship anyone can have with anything. When we know nothing, sometimes it can be because there is nothing to know: we are one with the world, and the world is one with us. It's called 'Buddha mind', the mind of 'oneness', and it's impossible to explain in words.

There are so many stories and koans of students seeking to understand this, and so many masters explaining, gently, that to understand the theory is not to understand the feeling. The statement 'mind is Buddha' is followed, neatly, by 'no mind, no Buddha'. We are looking to explain the inexplicable: the biggest things there are, and the smallest things there are. How can this be? How can we even contemplate something so strange and vast?

This is that Beginner's Mind again: this openness, this willingness to see the universe afresh every day. What is a raisin? What is a person? What can a person be?

Buddha urged his followers to have 'freedom from views' – something that can feel infinitely difficult in today's busy society. Surely we have to have views in order to know who we are? Surely if we want to know ourselves, we have to know our own views? After all, Buddha also urged his followers to commit only 'right actions' – and to have 'right views' – how can these things coexist? This is typical of the kind of questions studying Zen raises, and to answer it we have to come back down to first principles.

> Do I contradict myself?
>
> Very well then
> I contradict myself,
>
> (I am large,
> I contain multitudes.)

— Walt Whitman

Enlightenment

The first principle of Zen is that we are looking for *enlightenment*, and what that means is that we are looking to become ourselves *enlightened*: we are looking to truly understand, and truly learn, and that means it is not as simple as merely reading the answers in a little book and taking them to heart. It is for this reason that many Buddhists believe books to be 'dead words', and that the best way to learn is from a teacher — it's because having a teacher means that you, yourself, will have to practise. You, yourself, will have to show up; to sit, to think, to study.

Because, of course, when we say we're studying the universe, we're really studying ourselves — the only thing we can ever truly know. And learning ourselves takes a lifetime. We're always changing, and always growing, and every day we must begin again. We contain, as the poet Walt Whitman wrote, *multitudes*. We are the universe, and the universe is in each of us, and it is this that we must first consider when we consider Zen. It is this, in fact, that we must consider every day we consider Zen.

The great truths of the universe are the moon, and we are the still lake that reflects it; we can reflect it in small ways, and with our whole self. We can reflect the truth in tumbling fragments, like water spilling into cupped hands, or in a deep cool lake untouched by trouble. Both, I think, are worth having.

Enlightenment is like the moon reflected on the water. The moon does not get wet, nor is the water broken. Although its light is wide and great, the moon is reflected even in a puddle an inch wide. The whole moon and the entire sky are reflected in dewdrops on the grass, or even in one drop of water.

– Zen master
Eihei Dōgen

We Are One

The quote on the previous page lends us something else, too. It lends us this image of water, which we can borrow to understand a central Zen concept: that of *nonduality*. Nonduality, or *advaya*, means that everything is one, and that we are one with the universe; there is no second being. There is only one. We are droplets of water in a vast ocean, and only once we understand what that means and come together can we reflect the perfect image of the moon. We are one.

Take a moment, now, to sit with this idea. What does that conjure for you? Can you conceive of what this might mean? What it might look like in your life and in your heart?

The vast and complex universe are indivisible parts of a whole, and you – right now, reading this – are that whole; and so am I, writing this, and so are these words and every person – illustrator, editor, bookseller, so many others – who touched them between me speaking them to you right now, as you are. We are the whole, and we are one. We are connected, and this, too, is what the Buddhists mean by 'karma'.

Karma doesn't mean, necessarily, that you get out what you put in. It isn't, necessarily, a great cosmic balance sheet. It simply means that actions have consequences, like a stone tossed into a pond: things ripple out from the things we do, the things we are, and the things we think. I have learned from the people who taught me, and now I teach you, and perhaps you will teach others, and so the rings will spread ever outwards. The first teacher taught, and her student taught her student and so on, and here we are. We made this book for you so that we might pass on the things we have learned, and the ways we live, and your actions will perhaps be influenced by these things, and thus influence others. We are one; we are connected; we shape each other, change each other. We are one being, and so much of embracing Zen is trying to come to terms with this.

How can this be true? How can we exist fully in our bodies and in the world while we are also becoming one with all others? As always with Zen, one reaches the limit of the written word ('dead words' again), and so perhaps it is best to *show* you with an exercise.

The following exercise is called a 'body scan', drawn from one of the more modern approaches to Zen: mindfulness.

Mindfulness is an integral part of Zen meditation, and has taken on a life of its own. This exercise, often used in therapeutic practice, requires us to use the breath, as on page 46, to focus on each part of the body in order to achieve our full potential.

Full Body Scan

Sit comfortably, per the tips on page 42, and take a few deep breaths. Notice your breathing, as before. Acknowledge your breath, and respect your breath.

We're going to start by noticing how we feel, physically and mentally. How does your body feel against the floor? How do you feel about doing this exercise? Do you feel silly, or fidgety, or self-indulgent? Is your mind busy?

Breath by breath, we're just going to take note as if each one is the first breath we've ever taken. Really notice your breath; your pulse; the way your body rests against itself and the floor. Notice the way your breath feels in every part of your body, whatever that might mean to you. Can you feel your breath in your belly? Can you feel your breath in your shoulders, or your hips?

Now, we're going to draw this close attention into a singular focus: your little toes. How do they feel? Maybe you've never contemplated your little toes before – unless they hurt! – but now you can. Bring the attention into your other toes, too: your toes, arches, heels, ankles.

How does each part of your body feel? Is there pain or tension? Really concentrate on each sensation, or even lack of sensation. Bring your attention very slowly up the legs, through your calves and knees and thighs and hips.

This is all we need to do: just to concentrate on who we are, and how we are, right now. We're feeling our breath move through our body, and feeling our attention move up through our feet into our legs, and from our legs into our torso: back, belly, chest, noticing any sensations or even emotions. We're not trying to change anything: just noticing, and accepting.

Notice particularly any discomfort; notice feelings of discomfort. Move with purpose, and deliberately. Prepare to move before you move; prepare to scratch an itch, if you must scratch, by thinking through the movement before you make it. If you can, sit with the itch. Sit with the fidget or the pins and needles. Sit still, and think about it; consider it, consider the depth of discomfort. (Of course, don't put yourself into any danger. Merely consider whether you *really* need to move before you do so.)

Breathe in, breathe out. Your attention moves into your arms, your muscles, your elbows, your hands and fingers and fingertips.

Breathe in, breathe out. Move your attention slowly back up the arms and into the neck, the shoulders, the throat and chin and cheeks, the mouth, nose, eyes, ears and scalp. Each part of you is valid. Each part of you deserves attention.

When you're ready, open your eyes. Give yourself a moment or two to notice the world around you: the light, the atmosphere, the world to which you so indubitably belong, and which so indubitably belongs to you, neither seeking to know the other as both exist together, and are one. Notice how you feel: the connection, the peace, the one-ness…

The Four Noble Truths

The Four Noble Truths are the four truths Buddha learned in his life, and they are about suffering. They are, in fact, about freedom from suffering: they are about how to exist without pain, and the impossibility/possibility of that. They are hard for us to contemplate today, and as with so much in Zen teachings, sometimes they seem to take more than they give. Sometimes they seem impossible to apply to our own lives, and yet, in the next chapter, we'll consider them more carefully.

- **Dukkha**, the truth of suffering.

- **Samudaya**, the truth of the origin of suffering.

- **Nirodha**, the truth of the cessation of suffering.

- **Magga**, the truth of the path to the cessation of suffering.

4

Every Day Is a Good Day:

Zen and the Art of Suffering

There was once a Zen master named Ummon (or Yun-men), who lived more than a thousand years ago.

He was a wise man, famous for his eloquence and – sometimes – for his brevity. He hated to have his wise sayings written down to be sold. Yet many people have found deep truth in his oblique and strange stories, even though, as the Zen master Gyomay Kubose put it, his words 'talk about the south while looking at the north'. Like many Zen masters, he found solace in the strange and the obscure, and wisdom in things that might from another seem baffling or simple.

Many people came to hear him speak, a remarkable number of whom became enlightened. And one day Ummon came to speak to his followers, as usual, and he said: 'I am not asking you about the days before the 15th of the month. But what about after the 15th? Come and give me a word about those days.'

What does this mean? This is a koan, and like many koans is hard to parse at first sight. Come and give me a word about the days after the 15th of the month? What can that mean?

It might be useful to you, now, to sit a while – as discussed in the previous chapters – and think about it. Turn it over in your mind, ask yourself, live with it a minute. Let's sit together *zazen* and ponder this. *I am not asking you about the days before, but come give me a word about the days after.*

We can gain further insight by looking at another possible translation of this koan: *I don't ask about 15 days ago, but 15 days hence.*

You may come to your own conclusions: as with all koans, there's no one answer, but for me it means *live now*. It means live for the future, and not the past. It means change what you can change now, without recriminations for what you or others have done. Tell me where you're going, not where you came from.

And perhaps this seems to you to contradict other things you know about Zen, other things in this book – and perhaps it does. We can contradict ourselves, and contain multitudes; we can be many things, not just one thing. The Buddha is mind, the Buddha is not-mind; and we must come to each new moment with the Beginner's Mind, eager to learn again, and learn anew.

Because the story goes on:

And Ummon himself gave the answer for them: 'Every day is a good day.'

Let's bring this back to our *zazen* together, and think about what this might mean. Let's think about what this means in the context of suffering. Let's think about what this means in the context of a spiritual practice founded on the eternal truth of suffering.

(It can't be that Ummon, himself, was just having a particularly lovely life.)

Accepting Suffering

It seems, sometimes, that Buddhism – and by extension, Zen – is an unhappy religion, for it accepts at its core that suffering is the human condition (see the Four Noble Truths outlined on page 68).

It can seem, perhaps, a little unyielding; a little brutal to take this as the core of a new way of living. Frankly, even to discuss 'suffering' can feel both a little pretentious and a little unhelpful. Why would we dwell on this? Why would we use this acceptance of suffering as the basis of a new lifestyle?

When we think about this, we have to note first the difference between accepting the *fact* of suffering, and accepting suffering itself.

You see, even the briefest glimpse of life proves that suffering is part of the human experience: bad things happen to people, even good people. (In fact, mostly good people.) Many people's lives are full of terrible pain, and nobody's life is *free* from pain. All religions grapple with this. This is, perhaps, why people turn to religion or spirituality at all. Yet the difference between Zen and other traditions is this: in Zen, we can accept that the world is a hard one *without* blaming an individual for their own suffering, and *without* accepting that it has to remain that way.

If we are used to Western traditions, where pain is often a punishment, it can feel that this radical acceptance of suffering (and the way to escape suffering) is some kind of condemnation. If these bad things happen to us, surely we did something to cause them? If we are going to say that suffering is universal, surely we're condemning this whole world as morally 'bad'? But pain, in Zen, is not punishment.

Pain, in Zen, is merely a consequence of existence; and one we have to learn to understand and live alongside, and in this way we free ourselves from pain. This is a lot, I understand. This is hard to take in. It's almost another koan: we cannot free ourselves from pain, so to free ourselves from pain, we must live alongside the pain.

We have to live through the suffering, and embrace the suffering, in order to be free of the suffering. We have to live with it as if it were any other facet of the human experience: as rich and satisfying as joy, as worthwhile a teacher as love, and of course, essentially the same concept as both. Remember the previous chapter? There is only one thing. There is only one, and no other.

The Buddha believed there were three kinds of suffering: the suffering of unsatisfied desires, the suffering of constant change and the suffering of unenlightenment. Understanding these sufferings is the key to understanding Buddhist philosophy, which is the key to understanding Zen.

Unsatisfied Desire

Unsatisfied desire causes us suffering, because we want what we can't have. This doesn't mean simply material things – the house, the car, the designer clothes – but other things, too. Think back to the story of the Buddha on page 13, and the things he saw: the old man, the sick man, the dead. We desire material things, but we desire, too, to be young, to be well, for the dead to come back to life.

It's important to say, here, that it's the human condition to want these things. It can be hard to remember that this isn't an attack; it isn't saying, necessarily, that it is unreasonable to want. Merely, that this is a great cause of human suffering, and when you see this, it's easy to admit that it's true.

Constant Change

Constant change causes us suffering, because we want things to stay the same, lest we want what we can't have. We don't want things to pass away. We don't want to live in this endless cycle of rebirth, but the endless cycle of rebirth is what it is to be alive. This, too, is easy to admit. Things die, and other things are born; children grow up, and have children of their own; life comes in phases, and in waves, and with each new wave comes grief, even as it brings joy. It is hard to see time passing, sometimes: hard and strange, and painful, too.

Unenlightenment

And then we come to the last cause of suffering: lack of enlightenment, which is to say *not understanding*. Suffering comes from not understanding ourselves and our place in the vast universe. It comes from not understanding, truly, that there is no change; that what looks like change to an unenlightened mind is really just a small shifting of matter from one part of the whole to another.

It comes from not understanding that everything is interconnected. It comes from not understanding that we have everything we need, and everything we have is what we need: that our grief is someone else's joy, and vice versa, and that grief and joy and pain and love are all tied up together.

Anyone who has lived through anything can attest to that. We grieve for our loved ones because we loved them; we feel strangely sad when our children meet new milestones, even as we rejoice, because they will grow up and leave us.

So what can we do to avoid the suffering? How can we become enlightened, and how can we want only what we have? How can we live in the moment, and not in the past and the knowledge that this moment will soon become the past?

God, grant me the serenity
to accept the things
I cannot change,

courage to change
the things I can,

and wisdom to know
the difference.

– Reinhold Niebuhr

In so many traditions, in so many ways, we are seeking to answer the question of what can we do to avoid the suffering. It is, in many ways, the ultimate question – and that is what we are hoping to understand, by sitting *zazen* together. We are hoping to understand how to live mindfully and now. We are hoping to make every day a good day; every experience a new experience worth considering.

We are hoping to teach ourselves to understand intellectually what we do, secretly, know instinctively: we have only the moment. We have only now, and we have to live in it. We can only change how we respond to this ever-changing world: to follow our breath, to sit in peace and ease, to accept that joy and pain are two sides of the same coin, and to see that every day is a good day, if we let it be.

The Three Pure Precepts

These are, when you get right down to it, the aim
of Zen practice: these are the Three Pure Precepts for
which each person should strive their whole life. While
they may seem to say the same thing three times, each
one is worth meditating on separately: what is the
difference between doing no evil and doing good?
What is the difference between doing good and
deliberately doing good to others?

- We must do no evil.

- We must do good.

- We must do good *for others*, not just ourselves.

5

Wash Your Bowl:
Zen and the Physical World

Let's sit together *zazen*, now, at the end of this book. Let's contemplate the strange world we've travelled through together: all the stories that don't have beginnings and endings, all the contradictions and strange sentences that somehow add up to a whole. Let's sit *zazen* together and do a simple exercise: let's count to ten.

EXERCISE:

Count to Ten

Let's sit as we discussed early on (see page 42): comfortably and stably, as if we could sit for a long period of time, and let's try counting to ten. Count ten breaths, in and out – but only the breaths.

Each time you have a thought about anything that isn't your breath, stop, and begin again from one. Any time you notice anything but your breath, stop, and begin again from one. Any time you catch yourself thinking – even thinking about meditating, even thinking about counting, even thinking about numbers beyond the number you're on – stop, and begin again from one.

It feels impossible; in fact, for most people, it might be.

But this isn't about ten. It's not about reaching some arbitrary goal. It's about the moment, and the moment right now: simply about noticing your own thoughts, and acknowledging them – and, if you can, doing so joyfully.

Consider the Joys

We talked a lot, in the previous chapter, about suffering,
and by extension we talked about joy. I want us now – and
you, going forwards alone (although you're never alone with
nonduality) – to think about this the other way round.
I want us to consider the joys that are possible from living
in this way: the new joys that come from experiencing
a moment fully, with one-pointed concentration.

A sixth-century master, Fourth Chan Ancestor Chi'i, once
described the unenlightened as being 'like blind children of a
rich family sitting in a storehouse of treasures without seeing
any of them, just bumping into them when they move and
being wounded by them'. We want to open our eyes, to see
our treasures, and that is what the lifestyle described in this
book gives us the space to do. If we meditate, and do so daily
and regularly, we give ourselves space to understand the
things we have – not to covet more, or wish they lasted
longer, but to enjoy them as we have them.

Consider a bunch of peonies in spring: perfect as tightly folded buds, deep fuchsia in colour; perfect as they unfurl coral pink a day later; perfect as they drop cream-coloured petals and saffron-coloured stamens across the counter; perfect in memory; perfect even after the end in the knowledge that soon the summer will be coming into ripeness. In each stage the peony can be enjoyed; in each stage they bring us something new. In each stage they let us contemplate the present moment without wishing for more. You might think that this only holds true for beautiful things – and yes, it's easier when things are conventionally beautiful. But half the point of Zen is in finding that beauty wherever you see it, in simple things, in ordinary things.

Once a monk made a request of Joshu.

'I have just entered the monastery,' he said. 'Please give me instructions, Master.'

Joshu said, 'Have you had your breakfast?'

'Yes, I have,' replied the monk.

'Then,' said Joshu, 'wash your bowls.'

The monk had an insight.

Consider this koan for a moment: consider everything it says about a spiritual tradition that, far from being removed from the world and distant from our everyday cares, regards this conversation as worth recording. Think, in your next *zazen*, what it means to have transmitted this down the centuries, Joshu to monk, monk to his own disciples, and so on until I am telling it to you.

Have some breakfast. Do the dishes when you're done. This is the spiritual advice from Joshu, the great sage, author of many koans. Eat and wash up.

'A day without work,' said the great master Baizhang in the eighth century, 'is a day without food.' He was a sweeper and a farmer and a monk, and these are the people on whom this tradition is founded. Do your job, then sit, and find equal joy and spiritual satisfaction in both.

Think, too, of the setting of Joshu's koan – a monastery, where many people come. You owe it to them to wash your own bowl, to do your jobs simply and well: to not expect anyone to do anything for you that you would not with equal ease do for them.

Remember the third of the Three Jewels: the community. Remember the way that karma means you carry everyone else's decisions and actions and thoughts with you wherever you go, and they yours. Remember that we are all one. Remember that to bring our attention to one thing is to bring our attention to all things, and that to bring our spiritual attention to the act of, say, doing the dishes is to bring our attention to all acts. Humility, after all, is not humiliation: there is a dignity in these things, as there is dignity (aha!) in all things, and this is the great secret. There is dignity and Zen in all things; all things can be done as part of a Zen lifestyle.

When asked why he practised Zen,
the student said, 'Because
I intend to become a Buddha.'

His teacher picked up a brick
and started polishing it.
The student asked 'What are you
doing?' The teacher replied,
'I am trying to make a mirror.'

'How can you make a mirror
by polishing a brick?'

'How can you become Buddha by
doing zazen? If you understand
sitting Zen, you will know that

Zen is not about sitting or lying down. If you want to learn sitting Buddha, know that sitting Buddha is without any fixed form. Do not use discrimination in the non-abiding Dharma. If you practise sitting as Buddha, you must kill Buddha. If you are attached to the sitting form, you are not yet mastering the essential principle.'

The student heard this admonition and felt as if he had tasted sweet nectar.

– Zen master
Eihei Dōgen

It simply requires us to consider the 18 precepts scattered through this book, and to incorporate them into our lives with such diligence and dignity that they become second nature. Is this right? Is what I am doing right? Am I being the best version of myself? These questions, of course, are not new. They are common to all people – and all people may, given time, become Buddha. Buddha is in all of us, and Zen is possible for all of us.

The monk Joshu told to wash his dishes went on to write a poem, and it is four lines to turn over in your mind as you sit *zazen* next: four strange, obvious, disarming lines.

Because it is so very clear,

It takes longer to come
to the realization.

If you know at once
candlelight is fire,

The meal has long been cooked.

An Hachette UK Company
www.hachette.co.uk

First published in Great Britain in 2020 by Gaia Books,
an imprint of Octopus Publishing Group Ltd
Carmelite House
50 Victoria Embankment
London EC4Y 0DZ
www.octopusbooks.co.uk

Distributed in the US by Hachette Book Group,
1290 Avenue of the Americas, 4th and 5th Floors, New York, NY 10104

Distributed in Canada by Canadian Manda Group
664 Annette Street, Toronto, Ontario, Canada M6S 2C8

ISBN 978-1-85675-439-2

A CIP catalogue record for this book is available from the British Library.

Printed and bound in China.

10 9 8 7 6 5 4 3 2 1

Commissioning Editor Natalie Bradley
Art Director Juliette Norsworthy
Senior Editor Alex Stetter
Design and illustrations Abi Read
Assistant Production Manager Allison Gonsalves